BLUE BOO

and her Colorful Friends

A creative story and drawing book
for children of all ages

BLUE BOO
and her Colorful Friends

Also by Kathleen Whitmer

GREEN RUBBER BOOTS:
A joyful journey to wellness

FOR THE ASKING:
A joyful journey to peace

THE GLORY IN A STORY:
A joyful journey to making memories

TYPE DESIGN
Jotting, a self-published typeface by Santiago Salazar.

BOOK DESIGN AND PRODUCTION
By Peter Miller
Western Reserve Typographics, Akron, Ohio

PRINTING
BookMasters, Inc.
Ashland, Ohio

BLUE BOO

and her Colorful Friends

A creative story and drawing book
for children of all ages

Written and illustrated by
KATHLEEN WHITMER

Foreword by
DR. ELIZABETH FESLER, Ph.D.

PEACH PUBLICATIONS, INC.
AKRON, OHIO

BLUE BOO
and her Colorful Friends

A creative story and drawing book for children of all ages

Books may be purchased in quantity for educational, business or sales promotion use. Please write or call Peach Publications at the above address.

FIRST EDITION

ISBN 0-9661079-7-7

Library of Congress Cataloging-in-Publication Data:

      Whitmer, Kathleen.

      Blue Boo and her Colorful Friends

      Kathleen Whitmer. — 1st ed.

Library of Congress Control Number: 2007928217

Printed in the United States of America

This book belongs to:

_____

Aa Bb Cc Dd Ee
Ff Gg Hh Ii Jj Kk
Ll Mm Nn Oo Pp
Qq Rr Ss Tt Uu
Vv Ww Xx Yy Zz

DEDICATION

With grateful thanks I wish to dedicate this my fourth book to Jerry, my husband and to Peter Miller of Western Reserve Typographics, Akron, Ohio.

They have encouraged my work with positive and constructive ideas.

Jerry and Pete patiently listened as I wrote and planned.
Blue Boo went from being a dream to a reality under their encouragement.

Also thanks to my other big helpers:

Donamari Guy

Elizabeth Fesler, Ph.D.

Bill Wyatt

Patty Wyman

Peter Wilson

Lois & Courtney Gerstenmaier

And, finally, my sister, Mary Ann, who gave me the name Boo.

CONTENTS

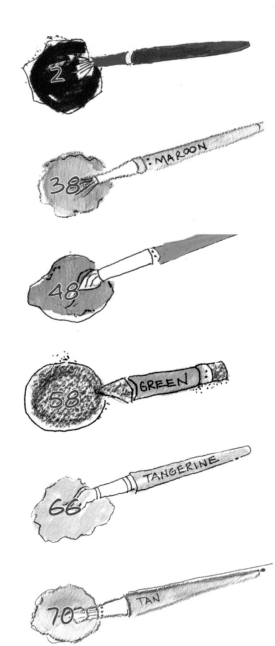

FOREWORD

Elizabeth Fesler, Ph.D.

To love the printed word, to get excited about a visual image is to jump start life long learning. This book will do that.

The artistic impulse is universal. Children throughout the world are all artists. They go through developmental stages: at two they scribble, but not randonly, at three the outline shapes, at four and five the drawn recognizable forms. They draw not for realistic scrutiny — they draw for their own pleasure.

This book, an elegant treasure to be shared with learners of all ages, presents wonderful possibilities inviting us all to become an active worker in continuing the story in words and drawings.

For centuries, humanity has applauded the process of artistry and other creative forms. Now, empirical data supports that and notes that the act of drawing develops higher level thinking skills like focusing, gathering information, remembering, and organizing. Howard Gardner views the arts as the most basic way of knowing.

Kathleen Whitmer engages the reader in consideration of the universal values of both relationships and inclusivity.

PREFACE

Blue Boo was written with color and tolerance as its two basic themes. Blue Boo is delighted to discover it would be fun to be blue.

Maroon June simply delights being with her maroon friend. Indeed, friends they be forever, you see.

Green Gene is so busy with his machines, he never gives being green a thought.

Red Fred is not as happy as the other friends of Blue Boo because his red color came from being in the sun.

Tangerine Maxine is a ball of energy. She makes everyone want to be just like she is.

Finally, Tan Dan, in his own creative way, grows up to be a great man after his happy days as a child playing in the sand on a beach near his home.

We need to work to be more tolerant of one another. What people are, on the outside, young or old, big or small, is not as important as what people are like on the inside.

Kindness	**Forgiveness**
Happiness	**Honesty and**
Joy	**Love...**

...all come from within our hearts.

Blue Boo is a story and drawing book for children of all ages. Clear, clean areas are provided to encourage the reader to draw his or her very own illustrations. There will be times when they will want to rest and return another time to draw and color and create pictures of Boo and her colorful friends.

Let the child's interest level lead in time spent on the stories and drawings.

It is my hope that Blue Boo will be among the readers most favorite books.

"We are all so different, yet, we are all so alike in many powerful ways."

Kathleen Whitmer
Author/Illustrator

BOO DREAMED SHE TURNED BLUE.

"TURN BLUE?" SHE ASKED WITH A GASP.

HOW LONG WOULD IT LAST?"

WOULD THE BLUE BE BRIGHT
OR WOULD IT BE LIGHT?

4

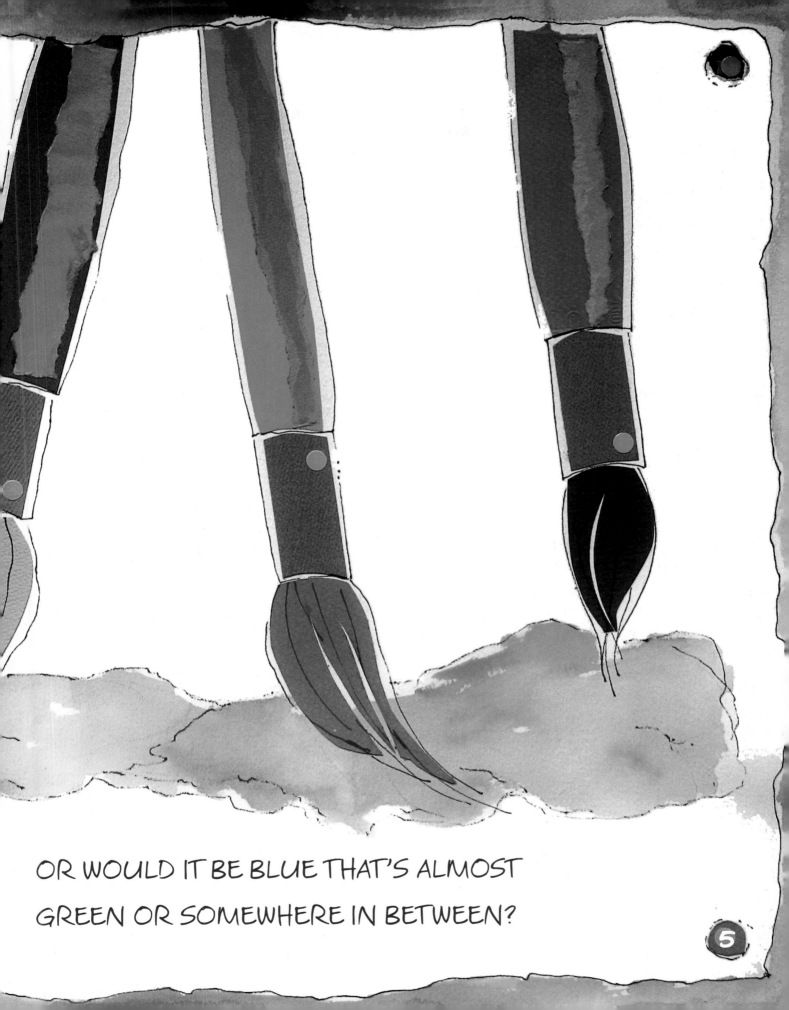

OR WOULD IT BE BLUE THAT'S ALMOST
GREEN OR SOMEWHERE IN BETWEEN?

BLUE AS DARK AS THE SEA OR DULL AS A GULL?
JUST WHAT COLOR WOULD BOO BE?

WOULD BOO TURN BLUE

FROM THE BLUEBERRIES SHE ATE, OR...

...FLYING THROUGH THE BLUE SKY SO GREAT?

OR WOULD WANDERING INTO THE BIG BLUE
YONDER TURN BOO BLUE SHE WONDERED?

DO YOU SUPPOSE THAT GAZING AT THE MOON EVER SO BLUE, OR LOVING THE HERONS OF BLUE BE A CLUE?

11

SADLY BOO WONDERED ABOUT TURNING BLUE
WHEN ONE DAY HER WORRIES WERE FEW.
WITH HER HEART ALL A FLUTTER...

SHE DREAMED OF A TRIP
TO THE BLUE BAYOU
WITH HER FAITHFUL AND
WONDERFUL DOG NAMED SUE...

...AND TO SWIM

WITH THE SILVERY BLUES.

HER HAPPINESS
ROSE AS HER BLUE SKIN GLOWED
"WHAT FUN TO BE BLUE,"
EXCLAIMED BOO.
"I CERTAINLY MATCH ALL
THE POPCICLES I EAT AND
THE COTTON CANDY SO SWEET!"

THE BEST PART IS OUT...

...A SECRET TO SHOUT!

...AND ONE OF A KIND HER FRIENDS ALL KNOW
FOR BOO NOW MATCHES
FROM HER HEAD TO HER TOE.

23

THE SCISSORS, THE SCRAPS,
ALL ANEW ARE BLUE!

25

HER DELIGHT THAT ALL CAN ENJOY

FOR THERE CERTAINLY IS NO PLOY

AN ARTIST SO TRUE

WITH A LIFE ALL ANEW

BOO NOW SIMPLY LOVES BEING **BLUE!**

Hi

Can you imagine what it would be like to be blue? It really doesn't matter what color we are on the outside, it's far more important what are like on the inside!

It might be fun to be blue. Blue is a wonderful color. It's the color of the sky and of ink. It's a friendly, happy color. Do you like blue as much as I do?

I hope you enjoyed **Blue Boo,** I liked writing it for you. Now I left some pages on which you may draw — have fun.

Love, Boo

CAN YOU DRAW YOURSELF AND SOME OF YOUR FRIENDS PLAYING HIDE AND SEEK WITH BLUE BOO?

CAN YOU DRAW BLUE BOO'S BEDROOM?

CAN YOU DRAW YOURSELF AS BLUE

BESIDE BLUE BOO?

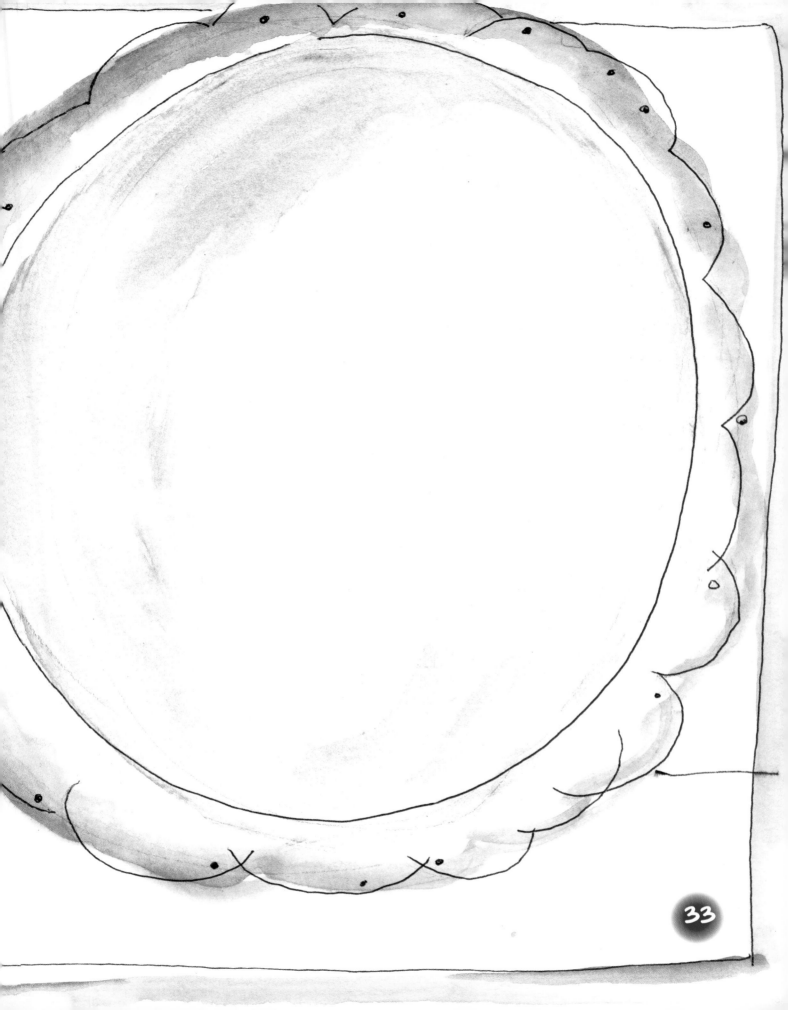

33

BOO STREET

BLUE ROAD

CAN YOU DRAW YOURSELF FLYING OVER
THE HOUSES ON BOO STREET?

MEET SOME OF BLUE BOO'S
COLORFUL FRIENDS.

MAROON JUNE

GREEN GENE

GLAD TO MEET YOU!

RED FRED

HI THERE!

TAN DAN

TANGERINE MAXINE

NOW YOU CAN LEARN MORE ABOUT EACH OF BLUE BOO'S COLORFUL FRIENDS

MAROON JUNE

MAROON JUNE
WAS FILLED
WITH GLOOM...
WHY WOULD
MAROON JUNE
BE FILLED
WITH GLOOM?

SHE SWEPT HER BEAUTIFUL ROOM
WITH HER BIG STRAW BROOM

SHE HAD FLOWERS IN HER GARDEN IN
FULL BLOOM THAT WOULD MAKE
A BOUQUET VERY, VERY SOON

HER MOTHER MADE HER ICE CREAM
THAT SHE ATE FROM A SILVER SPOON

AND, SHE EVEN HAD A BALLOON THAT
WAS MAROON

THEY WALKED ALONG THE STREET
    LOOKING SO NEAT

FOR THEM, LIFE LOOKED SO SWEET

THEN WHY WOULD MAROON JUNE AND
    HER MAROON BALLOON BE FILLED
    WITH GLOOM?

BECAUSE MAROON JUNE AND HER BALLOON
    WERE LONELY AS COULD BE

THEY HAD NO FRIENDS, YOU SEE

FOR MAROON IS A HARD COLOR TO BE

IF ONLY THEY COULD BE BLUE OR
GREEN OR EVEN RED, THEY SAID

IF THEY WERE YELLOW WOULD THEY BE MELLOW?

OR WOULD THE COLOR OF THE SEA FILL
THEM WITH GLEE?

WOULD ORANGE BE A MATCH FOR
EVERYONE'S EYE TO CATCH?

WERE PURPLE PEOPLE FILLED WITH GLOOM
WONDERED JUNE AND HER BALLOON?

WHITE SEEMED TRITE AND GRAY
SEEMED THE COLOR OF A BAY

PEOPLE GREEN, RED, YELLOW, PURPLE,   ENOUGH
FOR ALL TO SHARE BUT NONE OF THEM
SEEMED TO CARE

WITH HER BALLOON, JUNE DREAMED OF BEING
WITHOUT GLOOM WHEN SUDDENLY FROM OVER
THE HEIGHT SHE SAW A MARVELOUS SIGHT

FOR, TO HER SURPRISE, SHE WAS NOT THE ONLY
MAROON PERSON SHE WAS SOON TO REALIZE

A FRIEND TO HER WITH A BALLOON TO MATCH
THEY HUGGED AND THEY KISSED WITHOUT ANY
CATCH

FRIENDS FOREVER TO BE FOR COLOR MEANT
NOTHING, YOU SEE

GLOOM WAS NO MORE

THEY WERE FRIENDS FOREVER TO ADORE

BALLOONS TO LEND

SECRETS TO SEND

A FRIENDSHIP NEVER TO END

AND NOW WE SALUTE THIS FRIENDSHIP SO STRONG

IT WILL LAST VERY, VERY LONG

... AND NOW MEET **RED FRED!**

49

RED FRED

THIS IS FRED

FRED WILL SOON BE RED

"FRED WILL BE RED?

"FRED WILL BE REALLY RED," EVERYONE SAID.

THE DAY ALL ANEW

WITH A SKY SO BLUE

FRED WAS AWAKE BY EIGHT

READY TO SKATE

THE SUN SO BRIGHT, BIRDS IN FLIGHT

HE HAD FUN SINGING A SONG ALL DAY LONG

HIS FIRE ENGINE, RED AS COULD BE,

WAS FRED'S FRIEND ALL DAY, YOU SEE

RIDING UP AND DOWN THE STREET WAS A REAL TREAT

THE SUN SO HOT, ITS RAYS JUST SHOT

FRED DIDN'T KNOW

AS HIS DAY WENT SLOW

THAT THE SUN WAS NO FUN

AS AFTERNOON ROLLED ON

HIS WAGON, HIS SWING

EVEN HIS FRIEND'S BACKYARD

MADE SMILING HARD

HIS BICYCLE WHEELS SPUN 'ROUND

WHILE FRED WAVED TO ALL THOSE IN TOWN

AS HE PLAYED THE PART OF A CLOWN

HIS IRISH SETTER NAMED RED REACHED FOR A TREAT

"BOW WOW, YOU'RE RED AS A BEET!"

TIME TO GO IN FOR THE DAY

TOMORROW'S ANOTHER TIME TO PLAY

BEING RED WASN'T FUN AT NIGHT,

HIS WAS A SORRY SIGHT

HIS WAS A TERRIBLE PLIGHT!

IN BED FRED WAS RED

"IT HURTS TO BE RED IN BED," SAID FRED"-

HE LISTENED TO HIS MOTHER

WHEN HE LOOKED IN THE MIRROR

PROMISING NEVER AGAIN TO GIVE HER FEAR

A BASEBALL CAP

A LONG SLEEVED SHIRT

WOULD ALL BE THE THING

THEN PLAYING IN THE SUN

WOULD BE MORE FUN

FRED'S IS A MESSAGE

FOR ALL TO HEAR

BASEBALL CAPS WERE MADE

FOR MORE THAN TO CHEER

THE BILL ON THE FRONT

SHADES FRED'S FACE

SO NOW HE CAN PLAY AT A HEALTHY PACE

CAN YOU DRAW RED FRED IN THE SUN?

HIS LONG SLEEVED SHIRT
COVERS HIS SKIN
SO NO RAYS CAN GET IN
A WAY TO PROTECT HIMSELF
FROM THE SUN HAD BEGUN '

"I DON'T WANT TO BE RED EVER AGAIN!"
FRED EXCLAIMED

FRED'S LONG DAY OF PLAY WAS MORE FUN
FOR HE HAD LEARNED TO WEAR
HIS CAP AND HIS SHIRT
WHEN HE WAS IN THE SUN!

CAN YOU DRAW RED FRED IN HIS FIRE ENGINE?

DON'T FORGET TO PUT HIS SHIRT AND HIS
BASEBALL CAP ON HIM!

CAN YOU DRAW YOUR FAVORITE
SHIRT ON THE EMPTY PEG?

CAN YOU DRAW RED FRED'S HOUSE?

NOW MEET...

GREE

GREEN GENE WAS LEAN AS A BEAN
FROM THE SIDE HE COULD
HARDLY BE SEEN

GENE LOVED ALL KINDS
OF MACHINES

SOMEDAY HE'D BE A BUILDER OF
MACHINES, HE DREAMED

GEARS AND CHAINS,
STEEL AND BOLTS
HE WOULD MAKE A
MACHINE FOR
EVERYTHING PEOPLE HATE
TO DO THE MOST

...N GENE

HIS MOTHER COULD USE A DISHWASHER
    FOR SURE
    THAT WOULD SOAK AND SORT
    AND CLEAN SO PURE

WATER AND BUBBLES IN AND OUT
    WITH LOTS OF HOT AIR ALL ABOUT

THE DISHES SO CLEAN WOULD ROLL
    OUT THE DOOR
    AS THE MACHINE EVEN
    CLEANED THE FLOOR

AND IN HIS BEDROOM HE COUNTED
    HIS CHORES
    THERE WERE MANY HE DID NOT ADORE

LIKE MAKING THE BED, AND SCRUBBING THE FLOOR

HIS CLOSET WAS A DISASTER

HIS MOTHER THREATENED TO CLOSE IT

WITH PLASTER

HIS COLLECTION OF STAMPS

SAT UNDER HIS LAMP MESSY TO SEE

THEY SEEMED ALWAYS TO BE

GREEN GENE SAT DOWN, INDEED,

TO WRITE A LIST OF THE THINGS HE WOULD NEED

A MACHINE TO WASH DISHES GALORE AND TO SCRUB

THE FLOOR

ONE TO MAKE HIS BED WITH A

STRAIGHTENED SPREAD AND PILLOWS PUFFED

READY FOR HIS HEAD

A CLOSET CLEANER THAT WOULD SORT AND FOLD

SO EVERYTHING OF HIS IT WOULD HOLD

A SHREDDER, A COUNTER WITH BIG CLAMPS

WOULD ORGANIZE ALL HIS STAMPS

THE NEXT THING HE NEEDED TO DO WAS SHOP FOR THE
THINGS THAT HAD TO BE NEW

THEN TO THE SCRAPYARD
FOR TREASURES DISCARDED
FULL OF THINGS THAT MADE HIM HAPPY HEARTED

BOLTS OF ALL SIZES, BEAMS OF STEEL,
NUTS, SCREWS AND EVEN SOME REELS

IN HIS WAGON WOULD BE COMBINED
ALL THE THINGS HE COULD FIND
THAT OTHERS HAD LEFT BEHIND

ONCE HE GOT STARTED, IT WAS FUN, YOU SEE, FOR HIS
MACHINES FELL TOGETHER EASY AS COULD BE

THE DISHWASHER WAS FIRST ON HIS LIST
HIS MOTHER WOULD INSIST

A BRUSH CAME OUT FROM A SEAM
REACHING TO CLEAN THE FLOOR
AS THE DISHES HID BEHIND THE DOOR

MAKE THE BED
MACHINE

SORT MY STAMPS
MACHINE

CLOSET CLEANER
TO SORT AND FOLD

BUY SOME BIG CLAMPS
TO HOLD STAMPS

CLEAN CLOSET FLOOR
PUT SHOES IN ORDER

GREEN GENE BEAMED WITH JOY
   HIS MOTHER LOVED HER BOY!

HIS BEDROOM TOOK SHAPE
   HIS BED THE MACHINE DID MAKE
   HIS PILLOWS ALL PUFFED
   THE SPREAD SO STRAIGHT

IT ALL JUST SEEMED GREAT

HIS STAMPS WERE IN ORDER
   IN SIZE AND IN SHAPE
   TO SHARE WITH HIS FRIENDS
   A COLLECTION IT DID MAKE

THE CLOSET STOOD PROUD
   THAT EVERYONE SAID, WOW!

HIS CLOTHING SO NEAT
   SHOES LINED UP FOR HIS FEET

GREEN AND LEAN AS A BEAN
   GENE KNEW NO SCENE
   WHERE HE COULD NOT PLAN A MACHINE

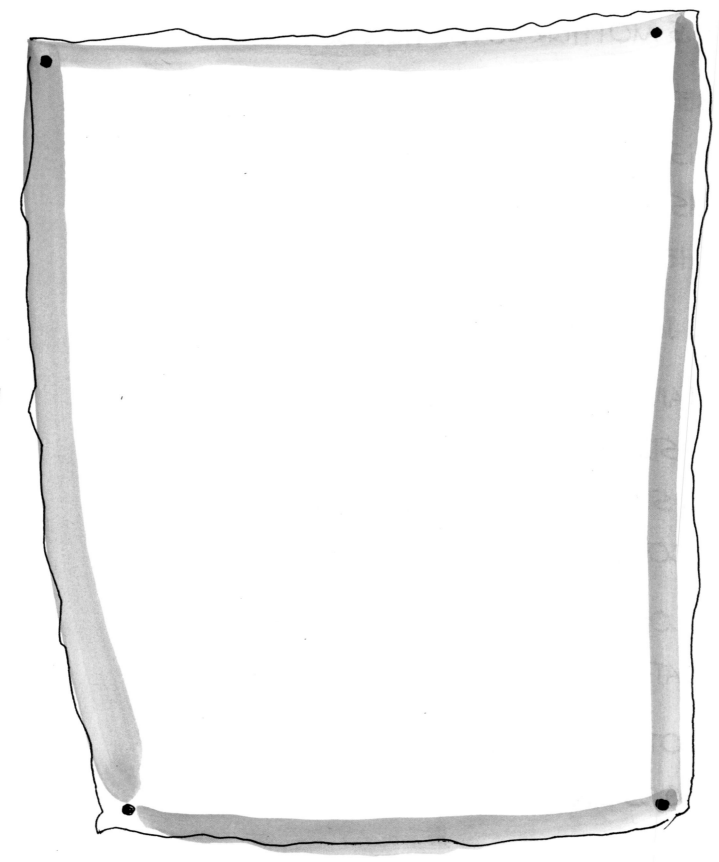

TRY DRAWING SOME OF GREEN GENE'S MACHINES!

IN ALL HIS HURRY AND RUSH
TO COMPLETE EACH MACHINE
SO LUSH AND SO PLUSH

GENE SUDDENLY REALIZED THAT
HIS MACHINES WERE ALL GREEN
AND THERE HE STOOD STILL
AS GREEN AND LEAN AS A BEAN
HAPPIER THAN HE HAD EVER BEEN!

TANGERINE MAXINE WAS A REAL BEAUTY
FROM THE CITRUS BELT
SHE WAS SURELY A CUTIE

SHE WORE BOOTS UP TO HER KNEES
WHITE PATENT LEATHER THEY WOULD ALWAYS BE

HER JEWELRY YOU WOULD NOT BELIEVE
IT WENT FROM HER FINGER TIPS TO HER
SLEEVES

67

RINGS AND BRACELETS GALORE
  FOR ALL HER FRIENDS TO ADORE

HER HAIR WAS RED WITH DARK SPECKLES
  AND HER FACE WAS DOTTED WITH FRECKLES

LAUGHTER WAS HER STYLE
  HER FRIENDS CAME FROM AS FAR AS THE NILE

THEY SANG AND DANCED
  JOKED AND PRANCED

TANGERINE MAXINE GLADLY TOOK CARE
  THAT HAPPINESS WAS EVERYWHERE

HER PHONE NEVER STOPPED RINGING
  EVERYONE WANTED TO CALL
  SHE WAS KIND TO ALL

SHE GLOWED A MARVELOUS GLOW
  THE WORLD WAS TO KNOW

68

CAN YOU DRAW TANGERINE MAXINE'S BEST FRIEND?

HER SECRET WAS EASY

HER SPIRIT WAS BRIGHT

SHE LAUGHED AND SMILED ALL THROUGH THE DAY

AND NIGHT

AND HER FRIENDS GATHERED AROUND

FROM ALL OVER TOWN

HOW HAS TANGERINE MAXINE MADE

SO MANY FRIENDS YOU WONDER?

THE REASON IS EASY AS THUNDER!

FOR TANGERINE MAXINE

KNEW NOT ONLY HOW A FRIEND TO HAVE, YOU SEE

SHE KNEW HOW A FRIEND TO BE.

HOW MANY OF TANGERINE'S FRIENDS CAN YOU SQUEEZE
INTO THIS SPACE?

TAN DAN LOVED TO PLAY IN THE SAND

    HE LIVED NEAR THE. BEACH

    AND, IT WAS EASY TO REACH

TAN DAN ALSO SWAM

    AS JOY FILLED EACH DAY

    IN THE WAVES HE DID PLAY

THE WAVES ROLLED IN AND OUT FROM THE MIDDLE

    WHILE DAN SWAM

    WITH THE EASE OF A FIDDLE

DAN SWAM LIKE THE FISH IN THE SEA

    NEVER BOTHERING TO WORRY

    WHERE HE WOULD BE

CAN YOU DRAW TAN DAN'S BEST SAND CASTLE?

THE FISH WATCHED FROM BELOW
        AS DAN DARTED FAST AND SLOW

LIFE NEAR THE SEA
        FILLED HOURS WITH GLEE

HE BUILT CASTLES IN THE SAND
        THAT WERE HUGE AND GRAND
        SOMEDAY HE WOULD BE A GREAT MAN

HIS CASTLES STOOD TALL
        BUILT STRONG NOT TO FALL

AS THE SAND TOOK SHAPE
        DOOR AND WINDOWS HE DID MAKE

DAN DREAMED OF BEING A MAN WITH A PLAN

THE MAN HE WOULD BE
        IT WAS EASY TO SEE

AS THE SAND TOOK SHAPE

    HE DREAMED OF THE BUILDINGS

    HE WOULD CREATE

SOME GREAT AND SMALL

    APARTMENTS VERY TALL

    SCHOOLS FOR ALL

A WORLD SO GREAT

    HE WOULD MAKE

WITH BEAMS OF WOOD AND FRAMES OF STEEL

    CITIES AND TOWNS WOULD BE REAL

TAN DAN'S TIME IN THE SAND

    HELPED HIM CARRY OUT HIS PLAN

    WHEN HE WAS TO BE A MAN

FOR, IT'S EASY YOU SEE

    AN ARCHITECT HE WOULD BE!

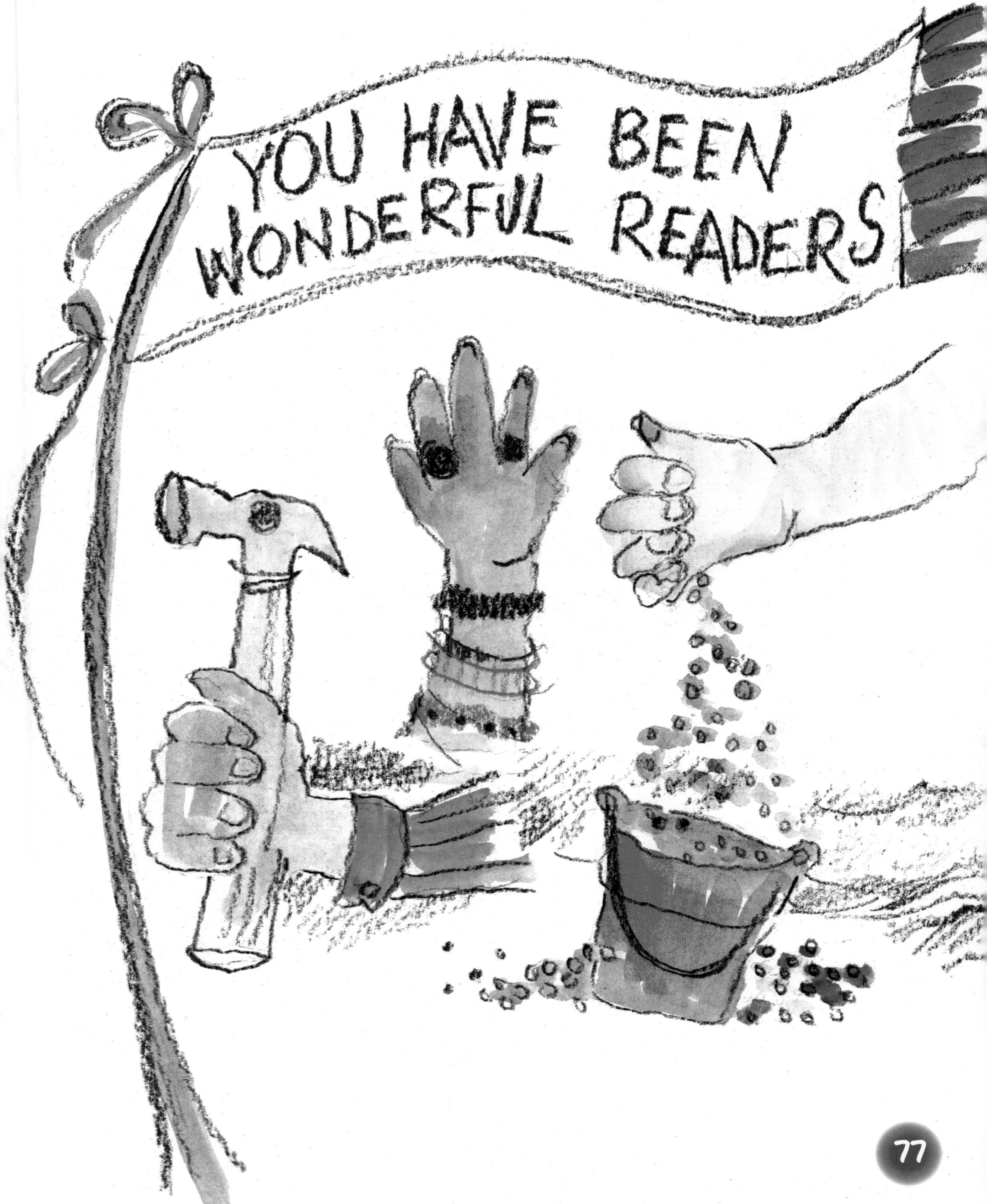
YOU HAVE BEEN
WONDERFUL READERS

We hope you liked meeting Blue Boo's
best friends. If ever you need a friend,
please feel free to drop a note to any of us:

Love,

Maroon June

Blue Boo

Red Fred

Tan Dan

Green Gene

Tangerine Maxine

We can be reached at:

Peach Publications

444 Burning Tree Drive

Akron, Ohio 44303

or

Fax 330-865-5650